FOOTBALL HEROES

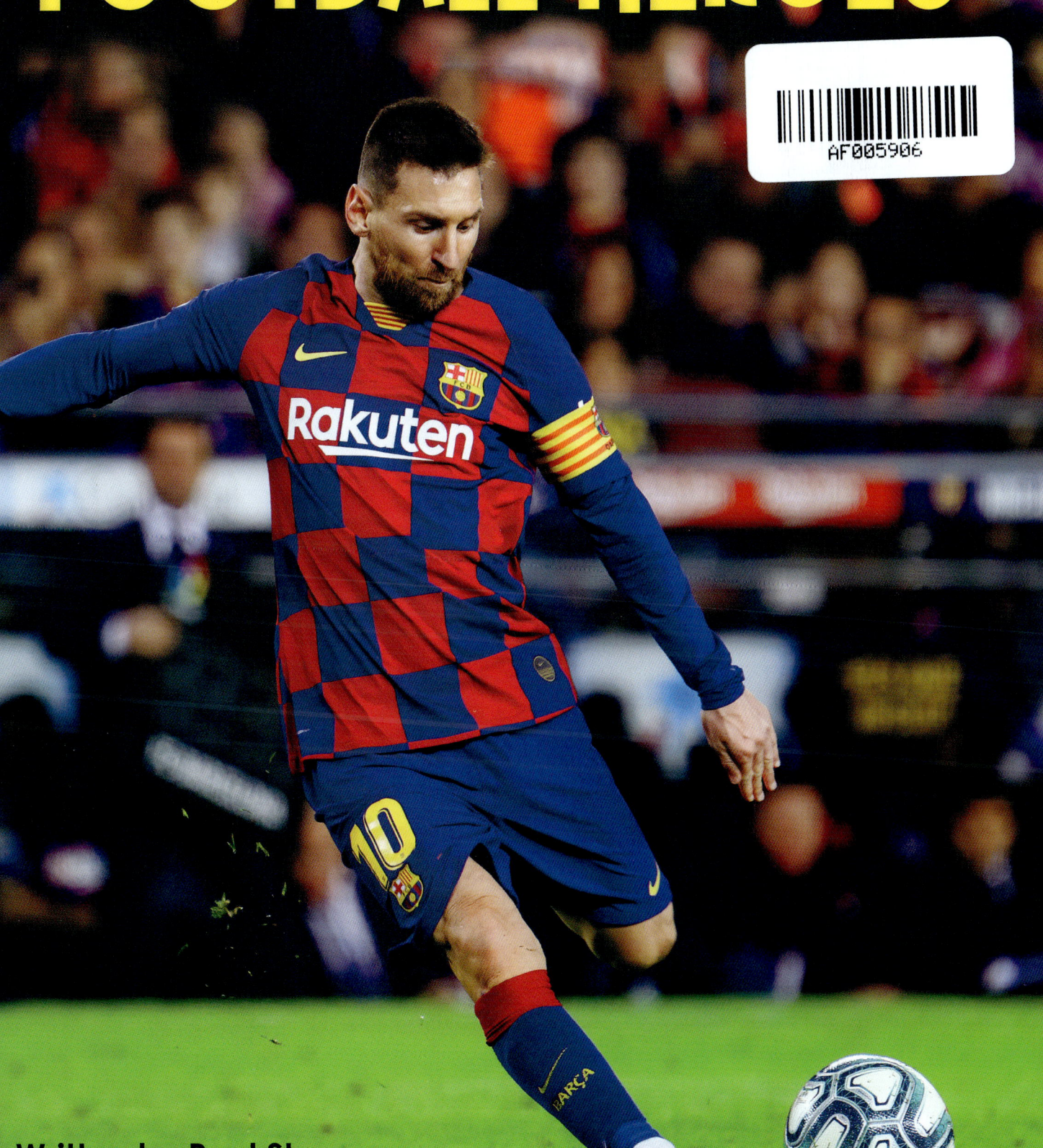

Written by Paul Stevenson

CONTENTS

Goal!	4
Early Heroes	6
Real Madrid	8
Manchester United	10
Pelé	12
Diego Maradona	14
Top Keepers	16
Top Transfers	18
Ronaldo v Messi	20
Marta v Prinz	22
Aitana Bonmati	24
USWNT Superstars	26
David Beckham	28
All-Time Greats	30
Glossary	31
Index	32

First published in 2024 by
Hungry Tomato Ltd
F15, Old Bakery Studios,
Blewetts Wharf, Malpas Road,
Truro, Cornwall,
TR1 1QH, UK.

Thanks to our editor, Julie Tofflemire.

Copyright © 2024 Hungry Tomato Ltd

No part of this publication may be reproduced, stored in a retrieval system, or transmitted in any form or by any means, electronic, mechanical, photocopying, recording, or otherwise, without prior written permission of the copyright owner.

A CIP catalogue record for this book is available from the British Library.

ISBN 9781835691229
Printed in China

Discover more at
www.hungrytomato.com

Neither the publisher nor the author shall be liable for any bodily harm or damage to property whatsoever that may be caused as a result of conducting any of the activites in this book.

All words in **BOLD** can be found in the glossary.

DISCLAIMER:
The moves and stunts featured in this book have been performed by experienced, highly-trained football players. Do not, under any circumstances, try them yourself.

GOAL!

Goals win games, but what does it take to be a true football hero?

1. TECHNICAL SKILLS

Football heroes are experts at controlling the ball. They pass and shoot with accuracy.

2. GAME INTELLIGENCE

Football heroes have incredible **spatial awareness**. They know where everyone is on the pitch and make quick decisions about the best play.

3. MINDSET

Football heroes have a passion for the game. They also keep their cool under pressure.

4. PHYSICAL SKILLS

Football heroes are strong and fast. They have excellent balance and **coordination**.

Who do you think is the top football hero of all time?

EARLY HEROES

Football as we know it today dates back more than 100 years, to 1863 in England. The sport has been producing heroes ever since!

DIXIE DEAN

Dean scored 60 goals in the 1927–28 season for English football club Everton. This was a record for the English **league**.

Dixie Dean

FERENC PUSKAS

In 1953, Puskas masterminded Hungary's 6-3 thrashing of England in the "Match of the Century".

Billy Wright, England

Ferenc Puskas, Hungary

JOHAN CRUYFF

Cruyff was the first player to be crowned "European Footballer of the Year" three times.

Cruyff had three goals and three assists in the 1974 **FIFA World Cup**.

BOBBY MOORE

Moore was an amazing **defender** and England's greatest-ever captain. He played 108 games for England.

Bobby Moore lifts the 1966 World Cup.

REAL MADRID

When it comes to legendary football clubs, you don't get any bigger than Real Madrid. The club once went 121 home games unbeaten!

As of 2023, Real Madrid have won the "La Liga" Spanish League a record-setting 35 times. They have also won 14 titles for the **UEFA Champions League**, more than any other club in history.

At the start of the 21st century, Real Madrid spent big to create a club of superstars. They were known as the "Galacticos".

WHO WERE THE GALACTICOS?

- Zinedine Zidane – France
- Luis Figo – Portugal
- Ronaldo – Brazil
- David Beckham – England

May 2022: Real Madrid players celebrate their Champions League win.

MANCHESTER UNITED

Manchester United is one of England's most followed football clubs. It was formed as Newton Heath Football **Club** in 1878.

CLUB STATS:

(Stats at the end of the 2022/23 season)
- 20 First Division / **Premier League** titles
- 12 **FA Cups**
- 21 **FA Charity Shields**
- 4 Europa League / Champions League titles

It's no surprise that Manchester United is widely supported around the world!

Wayne Rooney is Manchester United's top scorer of all time, with 253 goals!

Wayne Rooney

TRANSFER FEES:

First transfer fee: Gilbert Godsmark for about £40 in 1900.

Bargain buy: Peter Schmeichel (one of the best goal keepers) for the price of £530,000 in 1991.

Big money buy: Paul Pogba for an incredible £94.5 million in 2016.

Paul Pogba

PELÉ

Some say Pelé is the game's greatest-ever players.

Pelé was born into a poor family in Brazil. He shined shoes as a boy to make money.

He became the only player to win three World Cups – in 1958, 1962 and 1970.

"My name is Ronald Reagan, I'm the President of the United States of America. But you don't need to introduce yourself because everyone knows who Pelé is." - **Ronald Reagan**

PELÉ'S STATS
- Scored 1,279 goals
- Played 92 games for Brazil
- Played 656 games for Brazilian club Santos
- Played over 100 games for New York Cosmos

When playing for Santos, Pelé always wore the number 10 shirt. Santos retired the shirt when Pelé retired.

1974 - Pelé leaves the pitch after his final game for Santos.

DIEGO MARADONA

Maradona was one of Argentina's greatest-ever players. He scored 34 goals for Argentina.

He could weave past defenders with ease.

He was named the top player at the 1986 World Cup, which Argentina won.

In the 1986 World Cup, Maradona scored a **controversial** goal. From the referee's angle, it looked like a **header**. But Maradona used his hand to punch the ball into the net!

At the 1994 World Cup, Maradona was thrown out of the competition for his bad behaviour.

TOP KEEPERS

Every club knows the importance of a good goalkeeper. The keeper's lightning-fast **reflexes** and spectacular saves can make or break a game.

LEV YASHIN

Russian goalkeeper Yashin saved over 150 penalties in his career. He was known as "The Black Panther". Yashin retired in 1971.

ROGÉRIO CENI

Brazilian player Ceni wasn't just blocking goals – he was scoring them too! He scored more than 129 goals during his career, the highest of any keeper ever.

GIANLUIGI BUFFON

In 2001, Juventus bought Buffon for €52.9 million (£45 million), a record-breaking amount at the time. Most fans think he's worth it!

Buffon is the only goalkeeper to win UEFA Club Footballer of the Year.

IKER CASILLAS

Casillas is considered the best keeper in Real Madrid's history. He helped the club to take home five La Liga titles and three Champions League wins.

Fans call Casillas "San Iker" (Saint Iker) because of the **miracles** he performs on the pitch.

TOP TRANSFERS

Exceptional talent does not come cheap!
Clubs need big budgets to get the best players.

MOST EXPENSIVE TRANSFER: NEYMAR JR.

In 2017, Paris Saint-Germain paid an enormous €222 million (£190 million) fee for Neymar's transfer from Barcelona!

Brazilian player Neymar Jr. has scored more than 100 goals in his career. He's a playmaker and natural team leader with incredible speed.

Double the talent - Neymar is **two-footed!**

MOST EXPENSIVE TRANSFER FOR A TEEN: KYLIAN MBAPPÉ

In 2017, French 18-year-old Mbappé went on loan to Paris Saint-Germain (PSG) from Monaco. PSG sealed the deal in 2018 with a mega €180 million (£153 million) transfer fee!

During the 2015/16 season, Mbappé was Monaco's youngest ever player. This super striker has a powerful and accurate shot.

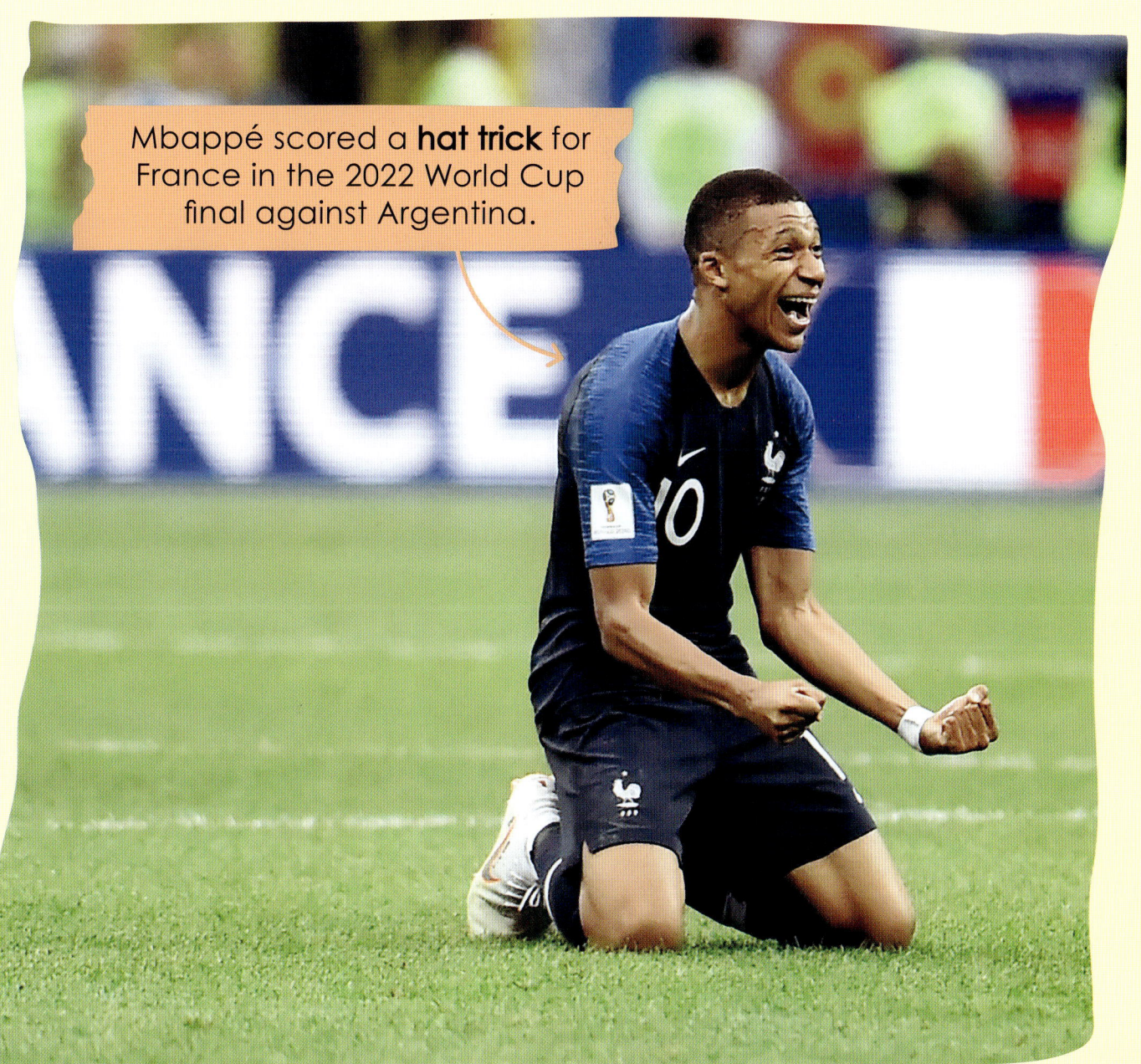

Mbappé scored a **hat trick** for France in the 2022 World Cup final against Argentina.

RONALDO v MESSI

Christiano Ronaldo and Lionel Messi are considered to be the best of the best. They are still playing and adding to their stats!

RONALDO'S RECORDS

Clubs: Manchester United, Real Madrid, Juventus and Al Nassr
Champions League wins: 5
Trophies: 35
Club goals: 759
International club goals: 128 goals for Portugal
World Cups won: none yet

Christiano Ronaldo transferred from Manchester United to Al Nassr in 2023.

Lionel Messi played for Barcelona, Spain, for 17 seasons.

MESSI'S RECORDS

Clubs: Barcelona, Paris Saint-Germain and Inter Miami
Champions League wins: 4
Trophies: 44
Club goals: 756
International club goals: 106 goals for Argentina
World Cups won: 1 (2022)

BOTH MAKE IT INTO THE TOP TEN FOOTBALLERS OF ALL TIME!

MARTA v PRINZ

Women's football has created its own legends.

MARTA VIEIRA DA SILVA'S ("MARTA") RECORDS

Country: Brazil

Clubs: Umeå IK (Sweden), Tyresö (Sweden), Orlando Pride (US) and more

International club goals: 115 goals for Brazil (as of 2022)

World Cup goals: 7 goals (top scorer in 2007 World Cup)

Awards: 7 FIFA World Player of the Year Awards (2006–10 and 2018)

Many football fans say Marta is the best women's player in the world.

In 2003, Prinz was offered a transfer to Perugia, a men's Italian **Serie A** club.

BIRGIT PRINZ'S RECORDS

Country: Germany
Clubs: FSV Frankfurt (Germany), Carolina Courage (US), FFC Frankfurt (Germany)
International club goals: 128 goals for Germany
World Cups won: 2 (2003, 2007)
Awards: 5 UEFA Women's European Championships

AITANA BONMATI

Midfielder Bonmati started playing for Barcelona when she was just 14 years old! She is a **versatile** player with great **vision**.

She scored three goals for Spain in the 2023 Women's World Cup, helping the club take home the victory. In her professional career, she has scored 93 goals (and counting!).

BONMATI'S CAREER HIGHLIGHTS
- FIFA Women's World Cup (2023)
- Women's World Cup Golden Ball (2023)
- 2 UEFA Women's Champions League titles
- FIFA Women's Player Award
- UEFA Women's Champions League Player of the Season

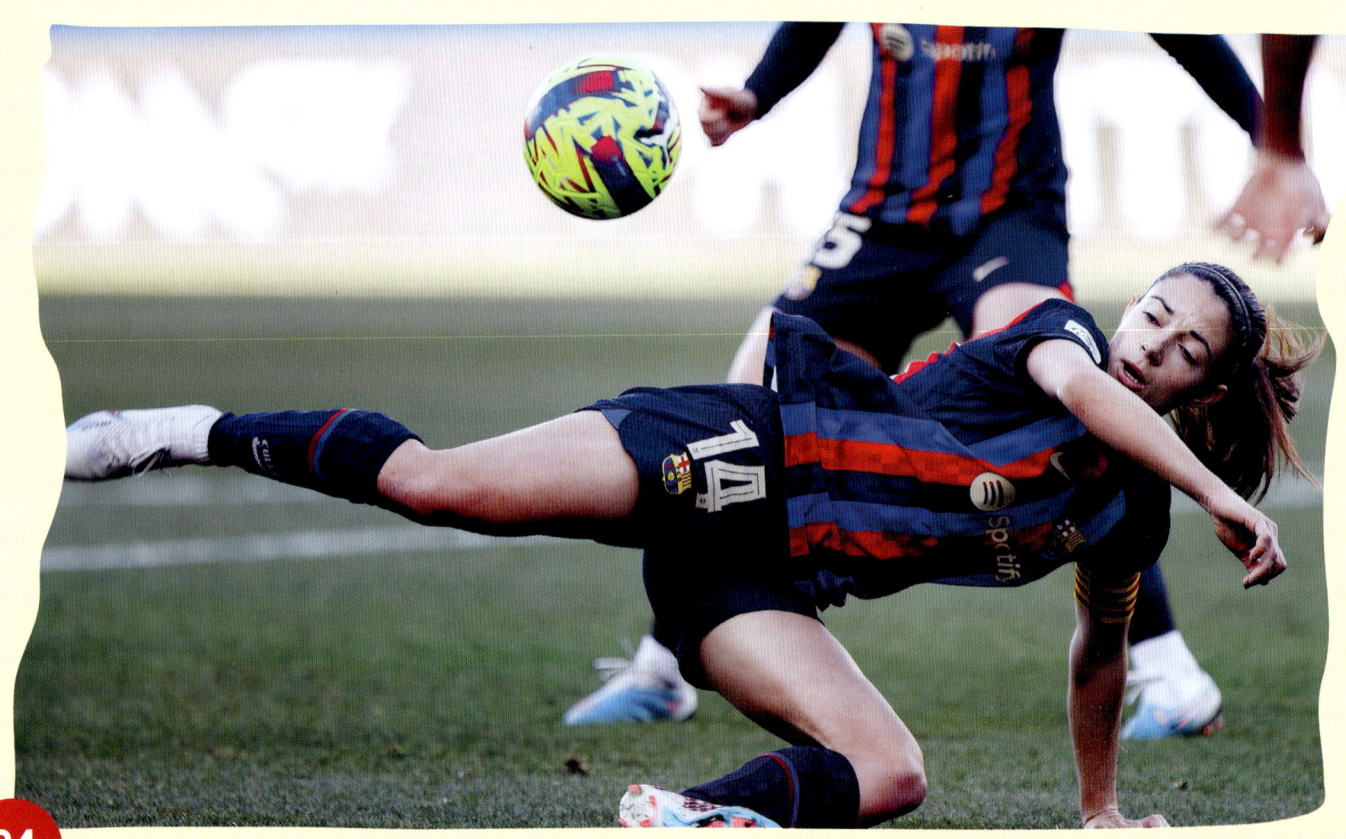

> "I have learnt that being resilient, never letting my head drop and working every day has its benefits."
> **- Aitana Bonmati**

USWNT SUPERSTARS

The United States Women's National Team (USWNT) won the first-ever Women's World Cup in 1991, and they just keep racking up wins!

USWNT is a dominant force in women's football. The speed and strength of the players are difficult to match.

USWNT RECORDS
- 4 Women's World Cup titles
- 4 Olympic gold medals
- 9 CONCACAF Gold Cups

USWNT club members celebrate their 2019 World Cup win

Mia Hamm (active 1987–2004) – a legendary **forward**, with an incredible 158 goals for the club.

Abby Wambach (active 2003–2015) – a record-breaking scorer, with 184 goals in 225 appearances.

Mia Hamm

Briana Scurry (active 1994–2010) – the first female goalkeeper and first African American woman to be added to the National Football Hall of Fame (US).

Crystal Dunn (active 2013–present) – a talented defender who adapts her play quickly.

Crystal Dunn

DAVID BECKHAM

David Beckham captained England's national club for six years. He is the only England player to score in three World Cups.

Beckham was famous for his swerving crosses and free kicks. His ability to bend the ball precisely and accurately was like magic. He once scored directly from a corner!

2008 - Beckham prepares to take a corner kick while on loan to AC Milan.

BECKHAM'S RECORDS
- 85 goals for Manchester United in 394 games
- 6 Premier League titles
- 2 FA Cups
- 2 FA Charity Shields

Major Clubs: Manchester United, Real Madrid, LA Galaxy, Paris Saint-Germain (PSG)

Messi

Beckham

Beckham is the co-owner of US football club Inter Miami, which signed Lionel Messi in 2023.

Messi is welcomed to Inter Miami

ALL-TIME GREATS

- In 1967, two armies that were at war in Nigeria stopped fighting for 48 hours. Why? To watch Pelé take part in a friendly match!

- Messi's international **debut** for Argentina lasted less than a minute! He was sent off after trying to shake off another player who was fouling him.

- Marta's family was poor, so they didn't have money to buy football balls. Instead, Marta used abandoned deflated balls or squeezed together shopping bags to make balls.

LEAGUE COMPETITIONS

- European Championship
- FA Cup
- FA Charity Shield
- FIFA World Cup
- Premier League
- Serie A
- UEFA Champions League
- UEFA Women's European Championships (a competition between the best national clubs in Europe. The competition takes place every four years.)

GLOSSARY

club – a football team.

controversial – causing a lot of disagreement and arguments.

coordination – the ability to control the movements of your body well.

debut – the first public appearance.

defender – a player whose main role is to stop the other side from scoring goals.

FA Charity Shield – a match played at the start of the English league season. It is usually played between last season's FA Cup winner and the League winners.

FA Cup – a very popular knockout competition for clubs in England and Wales. FA stands for Football Association Challenge Cup.

FIFA World Cup – (aka World Cup) an international football competition among senior national clubs held every four years. FIFA stands for Fédération Internationale de Football Association [International Federation of Association Football].

forward – a player whose main role is to stay close to the other team's goal and score goals.

hat trick – when a player scores three goals in the same game.

header – when a player hits the ball with his or her head.

league – a group of clubs who compete to win a championship.

miracles – incredibly amazing or outstanding events.

Premier League – the top level of English football.

reflexes – the power to respond or react with enough speed.

Serie A – the top football league in Italy.

spatial awareness – the ability to know or realise what is happening around you and where you are positioned in relation to other things.

two-footed – the ability to use both feet equally well.

UEFA Champions League – (aka Champions League) The Union of European Football Associations Champions League. The top football league for European countries.

versatile – able to do a lot of different things.

vision (in football) – the ability to spot passes and moves that other players are slow to see.

31

INDEX

A
AC Milan 28
Al Nassr 20
Argentina (team) 14, 19, 21, 30

B
Beckham, David 9, 28-29
Bonmati, Aitana 24-25
Buffon, Gianluigi 17

C
Casillas, Iker 17
Ceni, Rogério 16
Cruyff, Johan 7

D
da Silva, Marta Vieira 22-23, 30
Dean, Dixie 6
Dunn, Crystal 27

E
England (team) 6-7, 28

F
FIFA World Cup 7, 12, 14-15, 19, 20-21, 22-23, 24, 26, 28, 30-31
Figo, Luis 9
France (team) 19

G
Galacticos, the 9
goalkeepers 16-17, 27
Godsmark, Gilbert 11

H
Hamm, Mia 27
Hungary (team) 6

I
Inter Miami 21, 29

J
Juventus 17, 20

L
La Liga 8, 17

M
Manchester United 10-11, 20, 28-29
Maradona, Diego 14-15
Marta (see da Silva, Marta Vieira)
Mbappé, Kylian 18
Messi, Lionel 20-21, 29, 30
Moore, Bobby 7

N
Neymar Jr. 18

P
Paris Saint-Germain 18-19, 21, 29
Pelé 12-13, 30
Pogba, Paul 11
Prinz, Birgit 22-23
Puskas, Ferenc 6

R
Real Madrid 8-9, 17, 20, 29
Ronaldo, Christiano 9, 20-21

S
Santos 13
Schmeichel, Peter 11
Scurry, Briana 27

T
transfers 11, 18-19, 20, 23

U
USWNT (United States Women's National Team) 26-27

W
Wambach, Abby 27
World Cup (see FIFA World Cup)

Y
Yashin, Lev 16

Z
Zidane, Zinedine 9

Picture credits:
(t=top; b=bottom; m=middle; l=left; r=right):
AFP/Getty Images: 7tr, 16, 27m. Bob Thomas /Getty Images: 14-15bg. Getty Images: 13b. Marcus Brandt/epa/Corbis: 22-23bg. National Geogrpahic/Getty Images: 12m. Popperfoto/Getty Images: 6tr, 6b, 7b, 16mr. Shutterstock: Ph.Fab 9b, 29t, 30bl; YES Market Media 29bl; Paolo Bona 28b; Jose Breton – Pics Action 27br; Mikolaj Bar 26b, 31b; Christian Bertrand 21bg, 24b, 25bg; A.RICARDIO 19bg; A.Taoualit 18b; Maxisport 17br; Christiano barni 17m; Cosmin Iftode 11br; Jaggat Rashidi 11t; MDI 10b; Natursports 8b; Maciej Rogowski photo 2-3bg, 20bg; Anek.soowannaphoom 4-5bg.

Every effort has been made to trace the copyright holders, and we apologise in advance for any unintentional omissions. We would be pleased to insert the appropriate acknowledgements in any subsequent edition of this publication.